DOVER·THRIFT·EDITIONS

Shakespeare

A Book of Quotations

WILLIAM SHAKESPEARE

DOVER PUBLICATIONS, INC.
Mineola, New York

DOVER THRIFT EDITIONS

GENERAL EDITOR: PAUL NEGRI
EDITOR OF THIS VOLUME: JOSLYN PINE

Copyright

Copyright © 1998 by Dover Publications, Inc.
All rights reserved under Pan American and International Copyright Conventions.

Bibliographical Note

Shakespeare: A Book of Quotations is a new selection of quotations, first published by Dover Publications, Inc., in 1998.

Library of Congress Cataloging-in-Publication Data

Shakespeare, William, 1564–1616.
    Shakespeare—a book of quotations / William Shakespeare.
        p. cm. — (Dover thrift editions)
   ISBN 0-486-40435-8
   1. Shakespeare, William, 1564–1616—Quotations.   2. Quotations, English.
I. Title.   II. Series.
PR2892   1998
822.3'3—dc21
                                                                       98-31014
                                                                        CIP

Manufactured in the United States of America
Dover Publications, Inc., 31 East 2nd Street, Mineola, N.Y. 11501

Note

This was Shakespeare's form;
Who walked in every path of human life,
Felt every passion; and to all mankind
Doth now, will ever, that experience yield
Which his own genius only could acquire.
Akenside—*Inscription IV.*

William Shakespeare (1564–1616) wrote plays for a small English repertory theatre, a cooperative enterprise that enabled him to share in the financial success of his plays. He also acted occasionally— usually in secondary roles—and on the homefront was a landowning country gentleman. From this modest outline of a life emerged the greatest poet and chronicler of the human condition.

Because his muse was so often engaged in the participatory (vicariously or otherwise) genre of drama, his work flourishes in translation and transcends all boundaries of time and culture. In fact, his plays are more widely read and performed today than ever before. It is as if he mined a cosmic vein rich in the verities of human nature, forging his insights into grand and glorious art for the ages. By the force of his genius on the shape of our language, he helped form our very conception of ourselves. For at least partial proof of these statements, all one need do is examine the truth and ongoing relevancy of the quotations that follow.

In many instances, we routinely use these quotations almost intact, i.e., as they were originally written. For example: Clothes make the man; All that glitters is not gold; Neither a borrower nor a lender be; Gilding the lily; There's a method in his madness; and so on. In many other instances, however, usage through the centuries has changed their form, but on closer scrutiny seem nonetheless to reveal Shakespearean roots. To wit, from *King Lear*: "How far your eyes may pierce, I cannot tell; striving to better, oft we mar what's well" as in, "If it isn't broken, don't fix it." Then there's the ubiquitous, Kill the messenger (or, Don't kill the messenger, as the case may be), an expression perhaps deriving from: "Gardener, for telling me these news of woe, pray God the plants thou graft'st may never grow" (*Richard II*). There's even more than a little Karl Marx in Shakespeare, as demonstrated by this quote from *King Lear*: "Distribution should undo excess, and each man have enough." And evoking the latest scientific studies on the role of stress in the causation of illness: "I am sure care's an enemy to life" (from *Twelfth Night*).

The above is merely a very brief sampling of the contents of this volume, which is intended to provide revelation and inspiration for writers of all stripes, students and teachers, actors, and anyone else seeking an introduction to the wit and wisdom of one of literature's great visionaries.

Contents

Action	1	Madness	31
Adversity	1	Man and Woman	32
Age	2	Marriage	35
Ambition	3	Memory	37
Appearance	4	Moon	37
Bad News	5	Multitude	39
Beauty	5	Music	40
Conduct and Morality	6	Nature and the Seasons	41
Death	10	Patience	42
Destiny	12	Reason	43
Devil	14	Reputation	44
Drink	14	Sleep	45
Excess	14	Speech	46
Fashion and Apparel	15	Suicide	48
Fear	16	Suspicion	48
Forgiveness	17	Theatre	49
Human Condition	18	Thought	50
Jealousy	20	Time	50
Kinship	21	Truth	52
Law	21	Valour	53
Life	22	Various	54
Love	23	Wishes	57

ACTION

As many arrows, loosed several ways, come to one mark ... so may a thousand actions, once afoot, end in one purpose. *Henry V*, Act I, sc. 2.

✦

If it were done, when 'tis done, then 'twere well it were done quickly. *Macbeth*, Act I, sc. 7.

✦

What's done cannot be undone.
Macbeth, Act V, sc. 1.

ADVERSITY

Sweet are the uses of adversity,
Which like the toad, ugly and venomous,
Wears yet a precious jewel in his head;
And this our life, exempt from public haunt,
Finds tongues in trees, books in the running brooks,
Sermons in stones, and good in every thing.
As You Like It, Act II, sc. 1.

✦

Let me embrace thee, sour adversity, for wise men say it is the wisest course.
Henry VI, Part III, Act III, sc. 1.

A man I am cross'd with adversity.
> *The Two Gentlemen of Verona*, Act IV, sc. 1.

AGE

Young in limbs, in judgement old.
> *The Merchant of Venice*, Act II, sc. 7.

✦

My salad days, when I was green in judgement, cold
in blood. *Antony and Cleopatra*, Act I, sc. 5.

✦

Let me not live, after my flame lacks oil, to be the
snuff of younger spirits.
> *All's Well that Ends Well*, Act I, sc. 2.

✦

Crabbed age and youth cannot live together.
> *The Passionate Pilgrim*.

✦

You shall more command with years than with your
weapons. *Othello*, Act I, sc. 2.

✦

An old man is twice a child. *Hamlet*, Act II, sc. 2.

✦

The old folk, time's doting chronicles.
> *Henry IV, Part II*, Act IV, sc. 4.

✦

My age is as a lusty winter, frosty, but kindly.
> *As You Like It*, Act II, sc. 3.

Thou hast nor youth nor age, but, as it were, an after-dinner's sleep, dreaming on both.
Measure for Measure, Act III, sc. 1.

AMBITION

The very substance of the ambitious is merely the shadow of a dream.   *Hamlet*, Act II, sc. 2.

✦

I hold ambition of so light a quality that it is but a shadow's shadow.   *Hamlet*, Act II, sc. 2.

✦

Virtue is chok'd with foul ambition.
Henry VI, Part II, Act III, sc. 1.

✦

I have no spur to prick the sides of my intent, but only vaulting ambition, which o'erleaps itself, and falls on the other.   *Macbeth*, Act I, sc. 7.

✦

Lowliness is young ambition's ladder,
Whereto the climber-upward turns his face;
But when he once attains the upmost round,
He then unto the ladder turns his back,
Looks in the clouds, scorning the base degrees
By which he did ascend.
Julius Caesar, Act II, sc. 1.

✦

Ambition, the soldier's virtue, rather makes choice of loss, than gain which darkens him.
Antony and Cleopatra, Act III, sc. 1.

APPEARANCE

All that glisters is not gold;
Often have you heard that told;
Many a man his life hath sold
But my outside to behold.
>   *The Merchant of Venice*, Act II, sc. 7.

✦

Ornament is but the guiled shore to a most dangerous sea.   *The Merchant of Venice*, Act III, sc. 2.

✦

I have sworn thee fair, and thought thee bright,
Who art as black as hell, as dark as night.
>   *Sonnet CXLVII.*

✦

O, what may man within him hide, though angel
on the outward side!
>   *Measure for Measure*, Act III, sc. 2.

✦

There is no vice so simple but assumes some mark
of virtue on his outward parts.
>   *The Merchant of Venice*, Act III, sc. 2.

✦

Was ever book containing such vile matter so fairly
bound? O, that deceit should dwell in such a gorgeous palace!   *Romeo and Juliet*, Act III, sc. 2.

✦

Fair is foul, and foul is fair.   *Macbeth*, Act I, sc. 1.

✦

He takes false shadows for true substances.
>   *Titus Andronicus*, Act III, sc. 2.

BAD NEWS

Gardener, for telling me these news of woe, pray
God the plants thou graft'st may never grow.
Richard II, Act III, sc. 4.

✦

The nature of bad news infects the teller.
Antony and Cleopatra, Act I, sc. 2.

✦

Though it be honest, it is never good to bring bad
news: give to a gracious message an host of tongues;
but let ill tidings tell themselves when they be felt.
Antony and Cleopatra, Act II, sc. 5.

BEAUTY

Look on beauty, and you shall see 'tis purchased by
the weight.   *The Merchant of Venice*, Act III, sc. 2.

✦

Beauty is but a vain and doubtful good;
A shining gloss that vadeth suddenly;
A flower that dies when first it 'gins to bud;
A brittle glass that's broken presently:
    A doubtful good, a gloss, a glass, a flower,
    Lost, vaded, broken, dead within an hour.
The Passionate Pilgrim.

✦

Show me a mistress that is passing fair, what doth
her beauty serve but as a note where I may read who
pass'd that passing fair?
Romeo and Juliet, Act I, sc. 1.

Beauty provoketh thieves sooner than gold.
> *As You Like It*, Act I, sc. 3.

✦

'Tis beauty that doth oft make women proud; but,
God He knows, thy share thereof is small.
> *Henry VI, Part III*, Act 1, sc. 4.

✦

Those that she makes fair she scarce makes honest;
and those that she makes honest she makes very ill-
favouredly.   *As You Like It*, Act I, sc. 2.

✦

Sweetest things turn sourest by their deeds;
Lilies that fester smell far worse than weeds.
> *Sonnet XCIV.*

✦

O, she is rich in beauty, only poor that, when she
dies, with beauty dies her store.
> *Romeo and Juliet*, Act I, sc. 1.

✦

How much more doth beauty beauteous seem by
that sweet ornament which truth doth give!
> *Sonnet LIV.*

CONDUCT AND MORALITY

Neither a borrower nor a lender be:
For loan oft loses both itself and friend,
And borrowing dulls the edge of husbandry.
This above all: to thine own self be true,
And it must follow, as the night the day,
Thou canst not then be false to any man.
> *Hamlet*, Act I, sc. 3.

But screw your courage to the sticking-place, and we'll not fail.   *Macbeth*, Act I, sc. 7.

✦

How far your eyes may pierce, I cannot tell; striving to better, oft we mar what's well.
King Lear, Act I, sc. 4.

✦

I am a man more sinn'd against than sinning.
King Lear, Act III, sc. 2.

✦

Blow, blow, thou winter wind! Thou art not so un-kind as Man's ingratitude.
As You Like It, Act II, sc. 7.

✦

Rich gifts wax poor when givers prove unkind.
Hamlet, Act III, sc. 1.

✦

Condemn the fault, and not the actor of it?
Measure for Measure, Act II, sc. 2.

✦

Some rise by sin, and some by virtue fall.
Measure for Measure, Act II, sc. 1.

✦

Trust not him that has once broken faith.
Henry VI, Part III, Act IV, sc. 4.

✦

Vows were ever brokers to defiling.
A Lover's Complaint.

When he is best, he is a little worse than a man; and
when he is worst, he is little better than a beast.
                    The Merchant of Venice, Act I, sc. 2.

◆

I am constant as the northern star, of whose true
fix'd and resting quality there is no fellow in the
firmament.   *Julius Caesar*, Act III, sc. 1.

◆

How far that little candle throws his beams! So
shines a good deed in a naughty world.
                    The Merchant of Venice, Act V, sc. 1.

◆

No legacy is so rich as honesty.
                    All's Well that Ends Well, Act III, sc. 5.

◆

My ventures are not in one bottom trusted, nor to
one place.   *The Merchant of Venice*, Act I, sc. 1.

◆

I must be cruel, only to be kind.
                    Hamlet, Act III, sc. 4.

◆

Do not cast away an honest man for a villain's
accusation.   *Henry VI, Part II*, Act I, sc. 3.

◆

But to my mind, though I am native here and to the
manner born, it is a custom more honour'd in the
breach than the observance.   *Hamlet*, Act I, sc. 4.

Men's evil manners live in brass; their virtues we write in water.   *Henry VIII*, Act IV, sc. 2.

✦

The common curse of mankind,—folly and ignorance.   *Troilus and Cressida*, Act II, sc. 2.

✦

Foolery . . . does walk about the orb like the sun; it shines everywhere.   *Twelfth Night*, Act III, sc. 1.

✦

A stirring dwarf we do allowance give before a sleeping giant.   *Troilus and Cressida*, Act II, sc. 3.

✦

He hath eaten me out of house and home.
                    — *Henry IV, Part II*, Act II, sc. 1.

✦

Purpose is but the slave to memory, of violent birth, but poor validity.   *Hamlet*, Act III, sc. 2.

✦

Conscience does make cowards of us all, and thus the native hue of resolution is sicklied o'er with the pale cast of thought.   *Hamlet*, Act III, sc. 1.

✦

I know myself now; and I feel within me a peace above all earthly dignities, a still and quiet conscience.   *Henry VIII*, Act III, sc. 2.

✦

To do a great right, do a little wrong.
                    The Merchant of Venice, Act IV, sc. 1.

DEATH

Golden lads and girls all must, as chimney-sweep-
ers, come to dust.   *Cymbeline*, Act IV, sc. 2.

✦

A man can die but once.
                    Henry IV, Part II, Act III, sc. 2.

✦

He that dies pays all debts.
                    The Tempest, Act III, sc. 2.

✦

To be or not to be: that is the question:
Whether 'tis nobler in the mind to suffer
The slings and arrows of outrageous fortune,
Or to take arms against a sea of troubles,
And by opposing end them. To die: to sleep;
No more; and by a sleep to say we end
The heartache and the thousand natural shocks
That flesh is heir to,—'tis a consummation
Devoutly to be wish'd. To die, to sleep;
To sleep: perchance to dream: ay, there's the rub;
For in that sleep of death what dreams may come,
When we have shuffled off this mortal coil.
                    Hamlet, Act III, sc. 1.

✦

The undiscover'd country from whose bourn no
traveller returns, puzzles the will, and makes us
rather bear those ills we have than fly to others that
we know not of?   *Hamlet*, Act III, sc. 1.

Friends, Romans, countrymen, lend me your ears;
I come to bury Caesar, not to praise him.
The evil that men do lives after them;
The good is oft interred with their bones.

Julius Caesar, Act III, sc. 2.

✦

Ah, what a sign it is of evil life, where death's approach is seen so terrible!

Henry VI, Part II, Act III, sc. 3.

✦

Cowards die many times before their deaths; the valiant never taste of death but once.

Julius Caesar, Act II, sc. 2.

✦

When beggars die, there are no comets seen; the heavens themselves blaze forth the death of princes.

Julius Caesar, Act II, sc. 2.

✦

The sense of death is most in apprehension; and the poor beetle, that we tread upon, in corporal sufferance feels a pang as great as when a giant dies.

Measure for Measure, Act III, sc. 1.

✦

When he shall die, take him and cut him out in little stars, and he will make the face of heaven so fine, that all the world will be in love with night, and pay no worship to the garish sun.

Romeo and Juliet, Act III, sc. 2.

✦

Blow, wind! come, wrack! At least we'll die with harness on our back.   *Macbeth*, Act V, sc. 5.

DESTINY

Men at some time are masters of their fates: The fault, dear Brutus, is not in our stars, but in ourselves, that we are underlings.
Julius Caesar, Act I, sc. 2.

✦

As flies to wanton boys, are we to the gods; they kill us for their sport. *King Lear*, Act IV, sc. 1.

✦

We know what we are, but know not what we may be. *Hamlet*, Act IV, sc. 5.

✦

The gods are just, and of our pleasant vices make instruments to plague us. *King Lear*, Act V, sc. 3.

✦

O fortune, fortune! all men call thee fickle.
Romeo and Juliet, Act III, sc. 5.

✦

Some are born great, some achieve greatness, and some have greatness thrust upon 'em.
Twelfth Night, Act II, sc. 5.

✦

There is a tide in the affairs of men which taken at the flood leads on to fortune; omitted, all the voyage of their life is bound in shallows and in miseries.
Julius Caesar, Act IV, sc. 3.

Things without all remedy should be without re-
gard: what's done is done.   *Macbeth*, Act III, sc. 2.

✦

Full fathom five thy father lies;
    Of his bones are coral made;
Those are pearls that were his eyes:
    Nothing of him that doth fade,
But doth suffer a sea-change
Into something rich and strange.
                              The Tempest, Act I, sc. 2.

✦

A man may fish with the worm that hath eat of a
king, and eat of the fish that hath fed of that worm.
                              Hamlet, Act IV, sc. 3.

✦

Let Hercules himself do what he may, the cat will
mew, and dog will have his day.
                              Hamlet, Act V, sc. 1.

✦

Our remedies oft in ourselves do lie, which we as-
cribe to heaven.
                    All's Well that Ends Well, Act I, sc.1.

✦

Though fortune's malice overthrow my state, my
mind exceeds the compass of her wheel.
                    Henry VI, Part III, Act IV, sc. 3.

✦

Fortune, that arrant whore, ne'er turns the key to
the poor.   *King Lear*, Act II, sc. 4.

DEVIL

He must needs go that the devil drives.
                All's Well that Ends Well, Act I, sc. 3.

✦

He will give the devil his due.
                        Henry IV, Part I, Act I, sc. 2.

✦

The devil can cite Scripture for his purpose.
                The Merchant of Venice, Act I, sc. 3.

DRINK

O thou invisible spirit of wine, if thou hast no name
to be known by, let us call thee devil!
                        Othello, Act II, sc. 3.

✦

[Drink] provokes the desire, but it takes away the
performance.   *Macbeth*, Act II, sc. 3.

✦

O God, that men should put an enemy in their
mouths to steal away their brains!
                        Othello, Act II, sc. 3.

EXCESS

To gild refined gold, to paint the lily . . . is wasteful
and ridiculous excess.   *King John*, Act IV, sc. 2.

They are as sick that surfeit with too much, as they that starve with nothing.

The Merchant of Venice, Act I, sc. 2.

◆

Can one desire too much of a good thing?

As You Like It, Act IV, sc. 1.

◆

There's no bottom, none, in my voluptuousness: your wives, your daughters, your matrons and your maids, could not fill up the cistern of my lust.

Macbeth, Act IV, sc. 3.

◆

Speak of me as I am; nothing extenuate, nor set down aught in malice: then must you speak of one that loved not wisely but too well.

Othello, Act V, sc. 2.

◆

Distribution should undo excess, and each man have enough.   *King Lear*, Act IV, sc. 1.

FASHION AND APPAREL

Costly thy habit as thy purse can buy, but not express'd in fancy; rich, not gaudy; for the apparel oft proclaims the man.   *Hamlet*, Act I, sc. 3.

◆

The glass of fashion and the mould of form.

Hamlet, Act III, sc. 1.

Thou art not for the fashion of these times, where none will sweat but for promotion.
As You Like It, Act II, sc. 3.

✦

The fashion wears out more apparel than the man.
Much Ado about Nothing, Act III, sc. 3.

FEAR

Best safety lies in fear.   *Hamlet*, Act I, sc. 3.

✦

Present fears are less than horrible imaginings.
Macbeth, Act I, sc. 3.

✦

In the night, imagining some fear, how easy is a bush suppos'd a bear!
A Midsummer Night's Dream, Act V, sc. 1.

✦

Our doubts are traitors, and make us lose the good we oft might win by fearing to attempt.
Measure for Measure, Act I, sc. 4.

✦

His flight was madness: when our actions do not, our fears do make us traitors.
Macbeth, Act IV, sc. 2.

✦

To fear the foe, since fear oppresseth strength, gives in your weakness strength unto your foe.
Richard II, Act III, sc. 2.

FORGIVENESS

The quality of mercy is not strain'd, it droppeth as the gentle rain from heaven upon the place beneath. It is twice blest: It blesseth him that gives and him that takes.

The Merchant of Venice, Act IV, sc. 1.

✦

Sweet mercy is nobility's true badge.

Titus Andronicus, Act I, sc. 1.

✦

No ceremony that to great ones 'longs, not the king's crown, nor the deputed sword, the marshal's truncheon, nor the judge's robe, become them with one half so good a grace as mercy does.

Measure for Measure, Act II, sc. 2.

✦

Mercy is not itself, that oft looks so.

Measure for Measure, Act II, sc. 1.

✦

There is a devilish mercy in the judge, if you'll implore it, that will free your life, but fetter you till death.   *Measure for Measure*, Act III, sc. 1.

✦

Nothing emboldens sin so much as mercy.

Timon of Athens, Act III, sc. 5.

✦

Mercy but murders, pardoning those that kill.

Romeo and Juliet, Act III, sc. 1.

HUMAN CONDITION

O, that this too too solid flesh would melt,
Thaw and resolve itself into a dew!
Or that the Everlasting had not fix'd
His canon 'gainst self-slaughter! O God! God!
How weary, stale, flat, and unprofitable
Seem to me all the uses of this world!
Hamlet, Act I, sc. 2.

✦

There are more things in heaven and earth,
Horatio, than are dreamt of in your philosophy.
Hamlet, Act I, sc. 5.

✦

Oft expectation fails, and most oft there
Where most it promises; and oft it hits
Where hope is coldest, and despair most fits.
All's Well that Ends Well, Act II, sc. 1.

✦

Sorrow concealed, like an oven stopp'd, doth burn
the heart to cinders where it is.
Titus Andronicus, Act II, sc. 4.

✦

When sorrows come, they come not single spies,
but in battalions.　　　*Hamlet*, Act IV, sc. 5.

✦

The miserable have no other medicine, but only
hope.　　　*Measure for Measure*, Act III, sc. 1.

✦

It easeth some, though none it ever cured, to think
their dolour others have endured.
The Rape of Lucrece.

A heavy heart bears not a nimble tongue.
Love's Labour's Lost, Act V, sc. 2.

✦

Misery acquaints a man with strange bedfellows.
The Tempest, Act II, sc. 2.

✦

If there were reason for these miseries, then into limits could I bind my woes.
Titus Andronicus, Act III, sc. 1.

✦

How bitter a thing it is to look into happiness through another man's eyes!
As You Like It, Act V, sc. 2.

✦

Art thou not, fatal vision, sensible to feeling as to sight? *Macbeth*, Act II, sc. 1.

✦

Lord, what fools these mortals be!
A Midsummer Night's Dream, Act III, sc. 2.

✦

The fool doth think he is wise, but the wise man knows himself to be a fool.
As You Like It, Act V, sc. 1.

✦

Yet do I fear thy nature; it is too full o' the milk of human kindness. *Macbeth*, Act I, sc. 5.

✦

There is no fettering of authority.
All's Well that Ends Well, Act II, sc. 3.

Poor and content is rich, and rich enough; but riches fineless [i.e., infinite] is as poor as winter to him that ever fears he shall be poor.

Othello, Act III, sc. 3.

✦

Our purses shall be proud, our garments poor; for 'tis the mind that makes the body rich.

The Taming of the Shrew, Act IV, sc. 3.

✦

Present mirth hath present laughter; what's to come is still unsure.   *Twelfth Night*, Act II, sc. 3.

✦

A merry heart goes all the day, your sad tires in a mile-a.   *The Winter's Tale*, Act IV, sc. 3.

✦

Frame your mind to mirth and merriment, which bars a thousand harms and lengthens life.

The Taming of the Shrew, Induction, sc. 2.

JEALOUSY

O, beware, my lord, of jealousy! It is the green-eyed monster which doth mock the meat it feeds on.

Othello, Act III, sc. 3.

✦

Trifles light as air are to the jealous confirmations strong as proofs of holy writ. *Othello*, Act III, sc. 3.

KINSHIP

It is a wise father that knows his own child.
The Merchant of Venice, Act II, sc. 2.

✦

A little more than kin, and less than kind.
Hamlet, Act I, sc. 2.

✦

How sharper than a serpent's tooth it is to have a thankless child! *King Lear*, Act I, sc. 4.

LAW

The law hath not been dead, though it hath slept.
Measure for Measure, Act II, sc. 2.

✦

We must not make a scarecrow of the law, setting it up to fear [i.e., frighten] the birds of prey, and let it keep one shape, till custom make it their perch and not their terror. *Measure for Measure*, Act II, sc. 1.

✦

Do as adversaries do in law, strive mightily, but eat and drink as friends.
The Taming of the Shrew, Act I, sc. 2.

LIFE

To-morrow, and to-morrow, and to-morrow,
Creeps in this petty pace from day to day
To the last syllable of recorded time,
And all our yesterdays have lighted fools
The way to dusty death. Out, out, brief candle!
Life's but a walking shadow, a poor player
That struts and frets his hour upon the stage
And then is heard no more: it is a tale
Told by an idiot, full of sound and fury,
Signifying nothing.   *Macbeth*, Act V, sc. 5.

✦

All the world's a stage, and all the men and women
merely players.   *As You Like It*, Act II, sc. 7.

✦

The world's mine oyster, which I with sword will
open.   *The Merry Wives of Windsor*, Act II, sc. 2.

✦

I am sure care's an enemy to life.
      Twelfth Night, Act I, sc. 3.

✦

The web of our life is of a mingled yarn, good and
ill together.
      All's Well that Ends Well, Act IV, sc. 3.

✦

Life is as tedious as a twice-told tale vexing the dull
ear of a drowsy man.   *King John*, Act III, sc. 4.

And so from hour to hour, we ripe and ripe, and
then, from hour to hour, we rot and rot; and thereby
hangs a tale.   *As You Like It*, Act II, sc. 7.

✦

The cloud-capp'd towers, the gorgeous palaces,
The solemn temples, the great globe itself,
Yea, all which it inherit, shall dissolve,
And, like this insubstantial pageant faded,
Leave not a rack behind. We are such stuff
As dreams are made on; and our little life
Is rounded with a sleep.
                              The Tempest, Act IV, sc. 1.

LOVE

For aught that I could ever read, could ever hear by
tale or history, the course of true love never did run
smooth.
           A Midsummer Night's Dream, Act I, sc. 1.

✦

Let me not to the marriage of true minds
Admit impediments: love is not love
Which alters when it alteration finds,
Or bends with the remover to remove:
O, no! it is an ever fixed mark.   *Sonnet CXVI.*

✦

Perdition catch my soul, but I do love thee! and
when I love thee not, Chaos is come again.
                              Othello, Act III, sc. 3.

✦

O, then, what graces in my love do dwell, that he
hath turn'd a heaven unto a hell!
           A Midsummer Night's Dream, Act I, sc. 1.

O, how this spring of love resembleth the uncertain glory of an April day!
>>> *The Two Gentlemen of Verona*, Act I, sc. 3.

✦

Some Cupid kills with arrows, some with traps.
>>> *Much Ado about Nothing*, Act III, sc. 1.

✦

Love looks not with the eyes, but with the mind; and therefore is winged Cupid painted blind.
>>> *A Midsummer Night's Dream*, Act I, sc. 1.

✦

Love is blind, and lovers cannot see the pretty follies that themselves commit.
>>> *The Merchant of Venice*, Act II, sc. 6.

✦

If love be blind, love cannot hit the mark.
>>> *Romeo and Juliet*, Act II, sc. 1.

✦

If love be blind, it best agrees with night.
>>> *Romeo and Juliet*, Act III, sc. 2.

✦

What power is it which mounts my love so high, that makes me see, and cannot feed mine eye?
>>> *All's Well that Ends Well*, Act I, sc. 1.

✦

My mistress' eyes are nothing like the sun;
Coral is far more red than her lips' red . . .
I love to hear her speak, yet well I know
That music hath a far more pleasing sound.
>>> *Sonnet CXXX.*

Things base and vile, holding no quantity, love can transpose to form and dignity.

> *A Midsummer Night's Dream*, Act I, sc. 1.

✦

Speak low if you speak love.

> *Much Ado about Nothing*, Act II, sc. 1.

✦

I will wear my heart upon my sleeve for daws to peck at.

> *Othello*, Act I, sc. 1.

✦

Is love a tender thing? It is too rough, too rude, too boist'rous, and it pricks like thorn.

> *Romeo and Juliet*, Act I, sc. 4.

✦

The hind that would be mated by the lion must die for love.

> *All's Well that Ends Well*, Act I, sc.1.

✦

Self-love, my liege, is not so vile a sin as self-neglecting.

> *Henry V*, Act II, sc. 4.

✦

She cannot love, nor take no shape nor project of affection, she is so self-endeared.

> *Much Ado about Nothing*, Act III, sc. 1.

✦

Good night! good night! parting is such sweet sorrow, that I shall say good night till it be morrow.

> *Romeo and Juliet*, Act II, sc. 2.

Love lack'd a dwelling, and made him her place;
And when in his fair parts she did abide,
She was new lodged and newly deified.

A Lover's Complaint.

✦

But the strong base and building of my love is as the
very centre of the earth, drawing all things to it.

Troilus and Cressida, Act IV, sc. 2.

✦

All fancy-sick she is and pale of cheer, with sighs of
love, that costs the fresh blood dear.

A Midsummer Night's Dream, Act III, sc. 2.

✦

By heaven, I do love: and it hath taught me to
rhyme, and to be melancholy.

Love's Labour's Lost, Act IV, sc. 3.

✦

And ruin'd love, when it is built anew,
Grows fairer than at first, more strong, far greater.

Sonnet CXIX.

✦

When, in disgrace with fortune and men's eyes . . .
Haply I think on thee, and then my state,
Like to the lark at break of day arising
From sullen earth, sings hymns at heaven's gate;
    For thy sweet love remember'd such wealth brings
    That then I scorn to change my state with kings.

Sonnet XXIX.

This world is not for aye, nor 'tis not strange
That even our loves should with our fortunes change.
For 'tis a question left us yet to prove,
Whether love lead fortune, or else fortune love.

Hamlet, Act III, sc. 2.

✦

The chameleon Love can feed on the air.
The Two Gentlemen of Verona, Act II, sc. 1.

✦

Love's best habit is a soothing tongue.
The Passionate Pilgrim.

✦

There's beggary in the love that can be reckon'd.
Antony and Cleopatra, Act I, sc. 1.

✦

This thou perceivest, which makes thy love more
strong, to love that well which thou must leave ere
long.   *Sonnet LXXIII.*

✦

My bounty is as boundless as the sea, my love as
deep; the more I give to thee, the more I have, for
both are infinite.   *Romeo and Juliet,* Act II, sc. 2.

✦

Love's not Time's fool, though rosy lips and cheeks
Within his bending sickle's compass come;
Love alters not with his brief hours and weeks,
But bears it out even to the edge of doom.

Sonnet CXVI.

My love admits no qualifying dross.
Troilus and Cressida, Act IV, sc. 4.

✦

Alas, their love may be call'd appetite. No motion of
the liver, but the palate.
Twelfth Night, Act II, sc. 4.

✦

Who ever loved that loved not at first sight?
As You Like It, Act III, sc. 5.

✦

The ostentation of our love, which, left unshown, is
often left unloved.
Antony and Cleopatra, Act III, sc. 6.

✦

My love is strengthen'd, though more weak in
        seeming;
I love not less, though less the show appear:
That love is merchandised whose rich esteeming
The owner's tongue doth publish every where.
Sonnet CII.

✦

Doubt that the stars are fire;
        Doubt that the sun doth move;
Doubt truth to be a liar;
        But never doubt I love.
Hamlet, Act II, sc. 2.

✦

Where love is great, the littlest doubts are fear;
where little fears grow great, great love grows there.
Hamlet, Act III, sc. 2.

Against love's fire fear's frost hath dissolution.
                        The Rape of Lucrece.

◆

Love thrives not in the heart that shadows dreadeth.
                        The Rape of Lucrece.

◆

Friendship is constant in all other things
Save in the office and affairs of love:
Therefore all hearts in love use their own tongues;
Let every eye negotiate for itself,
And trust no agent.
            Much Ado about Nothing, Act II, sc. 1.

◆

If they love they known not why, they hate upon no
better a ground.   *Coriolanus,* Act II, sc. 2.

◆

Love's reason's without reason.
                        Cymbeline, Act IV, sc. 2.

◆

The expedition of my violent love outrun the
pauser, reason.   *Macbeth,* Act II, sc. 3.

◆

Ask me no reason why I love you; for though Love
use Reason for his physician, he admits him not for
his counsellor.
            The Merry Wives of Windsor, Act II, sc. 1.

◆

My reason, the physician to my love, angry that his
prescriptions are not kept, hath left me.
                        Sonnet CXLVII.

But miserable most, to love unloved? This you should pity rather than despise.
A Midsummer Night's Dream, Act III, sc. 2.

◆

Love sought is good, but given unsought is better.
Twelfth Night, Act III, sc. 1.

◆

Belike you thought our love would last too long, if it were chain'd together.
The Comedy of Errors, Act IV, sc. 1.

◆

If that the world and love were young,
And truth in every shepherd's tongue,
These pretty pleasures might me move
To live with thee and be thy love.
The Passionate Pilgrim.

◆

Love is begun by time; and that I see, in passages of proof, time qualifies the spark and fire of it. There lives within the very flame of love a kind of wick or snuff that will abate it.   *Hamlet*, Act IV, sc. 7.

◆

Now my love is thaw'd; which, like a waxen image 'gainst a fire, bears no impression of the thing it was.
The Two Gentlemen of Verona, Act II, sc. 4.

◆

Even as one heat another heat expels, or as one nail by strength drives out another, so the remembrance of my former love is by a newer object quite forgotten.   *The Two Gentlemen of Verona*, Act II, sc. 4.

When love begins to sicken and decay, it useth an enforced ceremony.   *Julius Caesar*, Act IV, sc. 2.

✦

Love surfeits not, Lust like a glutton dies;
Love is all truth, Lust full of forged lies.
                              Venus and Adonis.

MADNESS

Though this be madness, yet there is method in 't.
                              Hamlet, Act II, sc. 2.

✦

Madness in great ones must not unwatch'd go.
                              Hamlet, Act III, sc. 1.

✦

We are not ourselves when nature, being oppress'd, commands the mind to suffer with the body.
                              King Lear, Act II, sc. 4.

✦

How comes it, that thou art then estranged from thyself?   *The Comedy of Errors*, Act II, sc. 2.

✦

That way madness lies.   *King Lear*, Act III, sc. 4.

✦

Were such things here as we do speak about? Or have we eaten on the insane root that takes the reason prisoner?   *Macbeth*, Act I, sc. 3.

Matter and impertinency mix'd! Reason in mad-
ness!   *King Lear*, Act IV, sc. 6.

✦

Her madness hath the oddest frame of sense, such a
dependency of thing on thing, as e'er I heard in
madness.   *Measure for Measure*, Act V, sc. 1.

✦

Canst thou not minister to a mind diseased,
Pluck from the memory a rooted sorrow . . .
And with some sweet oblivious antidote
Cleanse the stuff'd bosom of that perilous stuff
Which weighs upon the heart?
                                    Macbeth, Act V, sc. 3.

✦

Fetter strong madness in a silken thread.
                Much Ado about Nothing, Act V, sc. 1.

MAN AND WOMAN

Sigh no more, ladies, sigh no more,
    Men were deceivers ever,—
One foot in the sea and one on shore,
    To one thing constant never.
                Much Ado about Nothing, Act II, sc. 3.

✦

There's daggers in men's smiles.
                            Macbeth, Act II, sc. 3.

✦

Let me have men about me that are fat,
Sleek-headed men, and such as sleep o' nights:
Yond Cassius has a lean and hungry look;
He thinks too much: such men are dangerous.
                        Julius Caesar, Act I, sc. 2.

His life was gentle, and the elements so mix'd in him that Nature might stand up and say to all the world 'This was a man!'

Julius Caesar, Act V, sc. 5.

✦

What a piece of work is man! how noble in reason! how infinite in faculty! in form and moving how express and admirable! in action how like an angel! in apprehension how like a god! the beauty of the world! the paragon of animals! and yet, to me, what is this quintessence of dust? man delights not me; no, nor woman neither.   *Hamlet*, Act II, sc. 2.

✦

What is a man, if his chief good and market of his time be but to sleep and feed? a beast, no more.

Hamlet, Act IV, sc. 4.

✦

Art thou a man? thy form cries out thou art:
Thy tears are womanish; thy wild acts denote
The unreasonable fury of a beast:
Unseemly woman in a seeming man!
Or ill-beseeming beast in seeming both!

Romeo and Juliet, Act III, sc. 3.

✦

He is the half part of a blessed man,
Left to be finished by such as she;
And she a fair divided excellence,
Whose fulness of perfection lies in him.

King John, Act II, sc. 1.

✦

However we do praise ourselves, our fancies are more giddy and unfirm, more longing, wavering, sooner lost and worn, than women's are.

Twelfth Night, Act II, sc. 4.

I have a man's mind, but a woman's might.
                        Julius Caesar, Act II, sc. 4.

✦

Men have marble, women waxen, minds.
                        The Rape of Lucrece.

✦

Men's vows are women's traitors!
                        Cymbeline, Act III, sc. 4.

✦

Give me that man that is not passion's slave, and
I will wear him in my heart's core.
                        Hamlet, Act III, sc. 2.

✦

Though men can cover crimes with bold stern
looks, poor women's faces are their own faults'
books.   *The Rape of Lucrece.*

✦

Women may fall when there's no strength in men.
                        Romeo and Juliet, Act II, sc. 3.

✦

A woman impudent and mannish grown is not
more loathed than an effeminate man in time of
action.   *Troilus and Cressida*, Act III, sc. 3.

✦

Age cannot wither her, nor custom stale her infinite
variety.   *Antony and Cleopatra*, Act II, sc. 2.

✦

Frailty, thy name is woman!   *Hamlet*, Act I, sc. 2.

Women, being the weaker vessels, are ever thrust to
the walls.   *Romeo and Juliet*, Act I, sc. 1.

✦

Have you not heard it said full oft, a woman's nay
doth stand for nought?   *The Passionate Pilgrim*.

✦

To be slow in words is a woman's only virtue.
          The Two Gentlemen of Verona, Act III, sc. 1.

✦

How hard it is for women to keep counsel!
          Julius Caesar, Act II, sc. 4.

✦

I thank God I am not a woman, to be touched with
so many giddy offences as He hath generally taxed
their whole sex withal.
          As You Like It, Act III, sc. 2.

✦

A woman mov'd is like a fountain troubled, muddy,
ill-seeming, thick, bereft of beauty.
          Taming of the Shrew, Act V, sc. 2.

✦

Were kisses all the joys in bed, one woman would
another wed.   *The Passionate Pilgrim*.

MARRIAGE

The ancient saying is no heresy, hanging and wiving
goes by destiny.
          The Merchant of Venice, Act II, sc. 9.

[Marriage is] a world-without-end bargain.
>*Love's Labour's Lost*, Act V, sc. 2.

✦

Men are April when they woo, December when they wed: maids are May when they are maids, but the sky changes when they are wives.
>*As You Like It*, Act IV, sc. 1.

✦

I will fasten on this sleeve of thine: thou art an elm, my husband, I, a vine.
>*The Comedy of Errors*, Act II, sc. 2.

✦

O curse of marriage, that we can call these delicate creatures ours, and not their appetites!
>*Othello*, Act III, sc. 3.

✦

By this marriage, all little jealousies, which now seem great, and all great fears, which now import their dangers, would then be nothing.
>*Antony and Cleopatra*, Act II, sc. 2.

✦

Though I want a kingdom, yet in marriage I may not prove inferior to yourself.
>*Henry VI, Part III*, Act IV, sc. 1.

✦

If there be no great love in the beginning, yet heaven may decrease it upon better acquaintance, when we are married and have more occasion to know one another . . . upon familiarity will grow more contempt.
>*The Merry Wives of Windsor*, Act I, sc. 1.

I have wedded her, not bedded her; and sworn to
make the 'not' eternal.

> *All's Well that Ends Well*, Act III, sc. 2.

MEMORY

When to the sessions of sweet silent thought
I summon up remembrance of things past,
I sigh the lack of many a thing I sought,
And with old woes new wail my dear time's waste.

> *Sonnet XXX.*

✦

Though yet of Hamlet our dear brother's death the
memory be green.   *Hamlet*, Act I, sc. 2.

✦

When wasteful war shall statues overturn,
And broils root out the work of masonry,
Nor Mars his sword nor war's quick fire shall burn
The living record of your memory.   *Sonnet LV.*

✦

I would forget it fain; But, O, it presses to my memory, like damned guilty deeds to sinners' minds.

> *Romeo and Juliet*, Act III, sc. 2.

MOON

O sovereign mistress of true melancholy.

> *Antony and Cleopatra*, Act IV, sc. 9.

✦

The moist star, upon whose influence Neptune's
empire stands.   *Hamlet*, Act I, sc. 1.

The moon of Rome, chaste as the icicle that's
curded by the frost from purest snow.
                              Coriolanus, Act V, sc. 3.

✦

What may this mean, that thou, dead corse, again,
in complete steel revisit'st thus the glimpses of the
moon?   *Hamlet*, Act I, sc. 4.

✦

The fortune of us that are the moon's men doth ebb
and flow like the sea, being governed, as the sea is,
by the moon.   *Henry IV, Part I*, Act I, sc. 2.

✦

The moon, like to a silver bow, new-bent in heaven.
        A Midsummer Night's Dream, Act I, sc. 1.

✦

But, soft! what light through yonder window breaks?
It is the east, and Juliet is the sun!
Arise, fair sun, and kill the envious moon,
Who is already sick and pale with grief,
That thou her maid are far more fair than she.
                        Romeo and Juliet, Act II, sc. 2.

✦

Swear not by the moon, th' inconstant moon, that
monthly changes in her circled orb, lest that thy
love prove likewise variable.
                        Romeo and Juliet, Act II, sc. 2.

The moon's an arrant thief, and her pale fire she
snatches from the sun.

Timon of Athens, Act IV, sc. 3.

✦

It is the very error of the moon: She comes more
nearer earth than she was wont, and makes men
mad.   *Othello*, Act V, sc. 2.

MULTITUDE

Ingratitude is monstrous, and for the multitude
to be ingrateful, were to make a monster of the
multitude.   *Coriolanus*, Act II, sc. 3.

✦

He's loved of the distracted multitude, who like not
in their judgement, but their eyes.

Hamlet, Act IV, sc. 3.

✦

The fool multitude, that choose by show, not learn-
ing more than the fond eye doth teach.

The Merchant of Venice, Act II, sc. 9.

✦

The beast with many heads butts me away.

Coriolanus, Act IV, sc. 1.

✦

The common herd.   *Julius Caesar*, Act I, sc. 2.

MUSIC

If music be the food of love, play on; give me excess
of it, that, surfeiting, the appetite may sicken, and so
die.   *Twelfth Night*, Act I, sc. 1.

✦

Music, moody food of us that trade in love.
                        Antony and Cleopatra, Act II, sc. 5.

✦

I can sing, and speak to him in many sorts of music.
                        Twelfth Night, Act I, sc. 2.

✦

Their savage eyes turn'd to a modest gaze
By the sweet power of music: therefore the poet
Did feign that Orpheus drew trees, stones and floods;
Since nought so stockish, hard and full of rage,
But music for the time doth change his nature.
The man that hath no music in himself,
Nor is not moved with concord of sweet sounds,
Is fit for treasons, stratagems and spoils.
                        The Merchant of Venice, Act V, sc. 1.

✦

To know the cause why music was ordain'd! Was it
not to refresh the mind of man after his studies or
his usual pain?
                        The Taming of the Shrew, Act III, sc. 1.

✦

In sweet music is such art: killing care and grief of
heart fall asleep, or hearing, die.
                        Henry VIII, Act III, sc. 1.

Though music oft hath such a charm to make bad
good, and good provoke to harm.
                    Measure for Measure, Act IV, sc. 1.

NATURE AND THE SEASONS

Nature does require her times of preservation.
                    Henry VIII, Act III, sc. 2.

✦

Winter, which, being full of care, makes summer's
welcome thrice more wish'd, more rare.
                    Sonnet LVI.

✦

Beware the ides of March.
                    Julius Caesar, Act I, sc. 2.

✦

Under the greenwood tree who loves to lie with me
. . . Here shall he see no enemy but winter and
rough weather.   *As You Like It*, Act II, sc. 5.

✦

In the spring time, the only pretty ring time, when
birds do sing . . . sweet lovers love the spring.
                    As You Like It, Act V, sc. 3.

✦

        Where the bee sucks, there suck I:
        In a cowslip's bell I lie;
        There I couch when owls do cry.
        On the bat's back I do fly
        After summer merrily.
Merrily, merrily shall I live now
Under the blossom that hangs on the bough.
                    The Tempest, Act V, sc. 1.

Shall I compare thee to a summer's day?
Thou art more lovely and more temperate:
Rough winds do shake the darling buds of May,
And summer's lease hath all too short a date.

Sonnet XVIII.

✦

Why, this is very midsummer madness.

Twelfth Night, Act III, sc. 4.

✦

That time of year thou may'st in me behold,
When yellow leaves, or none, or few, do hang
Upon those boughs which shake against the cold,—
Bare ruin'd choirs, where late the sweet birds sang.

Sonnet LXXIII.

✦

Now is the winter of our discontent
Made glorious summer by this sun of York,
And all the clouds that loured upon our house
In the deep bosom of the ocean buried.

Richard III, Act I, sc. 1.

PATIENCE

A very little thief of occasion will rob you of a great
deal of patience.   *Coriolanus*, Act II, sc. 1.

✦

Patience is sottish, and impatience does become a
dog that's mad.

Antony and Cleopatra, Act IV, sc. 15.

I do oppose my patience to his fury, and am arm'd
to suffer with a quietness of spirit, the very tyranny
and rage of his.
                    The Merchant of Venice, Act IV, sc. 1.

❖

Upon the heat and flame of thy distemper sprinkle
cool patience.   *Hamlet*, Act III, sc. 4.

❖

How poor are they that have not patience! What
wound did ever heal but by degrees?
                    Othello, Act II, sc. 3.

❖

Though patience be a tired mare, yet she will plod.
                    Henry V, Act II, sc. 1.

❖

Had it pleas'd heaven to try me with affliction . . .
I should have found in some place of my soul a drop
of patience.   *Othello*, Act IV, sc. 2.

❖

A high hope for a low heaven: God grant us
patience!   *Love's Labour's Lost*, Act I, sc. 1.

REASON

Sure, he that made us with such large discourse,
looking before and after, gave us not that capability
and god-like reason to fust in us unus'd.
                    Hamlet, Act IV, sc. 4.

❖

Every why hath a wherefore.
                    The Comedy of Errors, Act II, sc. 2.

Strong reasons make strong actions.
>>> *King John*, Act III, sc. 4.

◆

His reasons are as two grains of wheat hid in two bushels of chaff: you shall seek all day ere you find them, and when you have them, they are not worth the search.   *The Merchant of Venice*, Act I, sc. 1.

◆

Do not banish reason for inequality; but let your reason serve to make the truth appear where it seems hid, and hide the false seems true.
>>> *Measure for Measure*, Act V, sc. 1.

◆

Many that are not mad have, sure, more lack of reason.   *Measure for Measure*, Act V, sc. 1.

REPUTATION

Oh, I have lost my reputation! I have lost the immortal part of myself, and what remains is bestial.
>>> *Othello*, Act II, sc. 3.

◆

Good name in man and woman, dear my lord,
Is the immediate jewel of their souls:
Who steals my purse steals trash; 'tis something, nothing;
'Twas mine, 'tis his, and has been slave to thousands;
But he that filches from me my good name
Robs me of that which not enriches him
And makes me poor indeed. *Othello*, Act III, sc. 3.

The purest treasure mortal times afford is spotless reputation; that away, men are but gilded loam or painted clay.   *Richard II*, Act I, sc. 1.

✦

Reputation is an idle and most false imposition; oft got without merit, and lost without deserving.
                                        Othello, Act II, sc. 3.

SLEEP

Sleep that knits up the ravell'd sleave of care, the death of each day's life, sore labour's bath, balm of hurt minds, great nature's second course, chief nourisher in life's feast.   *Macbeth*, Act II, sc. 2.

✦

O sleep, thou ape of death, lie dull upon her and be her sense but as a monument, thus in a chapel lying.   *Cymbeline*, Act II, sc. 2.

✦

A great perturbation in nature, to receive at once the benefit of sleep and do the effects of watching!
                                        Macbeth, Act V, sc. 1.

✦

Shake off this downy sleep, death's counterfeit, and look on death itself!   *Macbeth*, Act II, sc. 3.

✦

Methought I heard a voice cry, "Sleep no more! Macbeth does murder sleep!"—the innocent sleep.
                                        Macbeth, Act II, sc. 2.

O sleep, O gentle sleep, nature's soft nurse,
how have I frighted thee, that thou no more
wilt weigh my eyelids down, and steep my senses in
forgetfulness?   *Henry IV, Part II*, Act III, sc. 1.

✦

Sleep, that sometimes shuts up sorrow's eye, steal
me awhile from mine own company.
            A Midsummer Night's Dream, Act III, sc. 2.

✦

Care keeps his watch in every old man's eye,
And where care lodges, sleep will never lie;
But where unbruised youth with unstuff'd brain
Doth couch his limbs, there golden sleep doth reign.
            Romeo and Juliet, Act II, sc. 3.

✦

He that sleeps feels not the tooth-ache.
            Cymbeline, Act V, sc. 4.

SPEECH

Brevity is the soul of wit.
            Hamlet, Act II, sc. 2.

✦

Men of few words are the best men.
            Henry V, Act III, sc. 2.

✦

I do know of these that . . . only are reputed wise for
saying nothing.
            The Merchant of Venice, Act I, sc. 1.

Talkers are no good doers; be assur'd we come to
use our hands and not our tongues.
                            Richard III, Act I, sc. 3.

✦

Be check'd for silence, but never tax'd for speech.
            All's Well that Ends Well, Act I, sc. 1.

✦

How absolute the knave is! we must speak by the
card, or equivocation will undo us.
                            Hamlet, Act V, sc. 1.

✦

I do not speak to thee in drink but in tears, not in
pleasure but in passion, not in words only, but in
woes also.   *Henry IV, Part I*, Act II, sc. 4.

✦

Weighest thy words before thou givest them breath.
                            Othello, Act III, sc. 3.

✦

Ill deeds are doubled with an evil word.
                    The Comedy of Errors, Act III, sc. 2.

✦

Things are often spoke and seldom meant.
                    Henry VI, Part II, Act III, sc. 1.

✦

Be it art or hap, he hath spoken true.
                    Antony and Cleopatra, Act II, sc. 3.

✦

Though thou speakest truth, methink thou speak'st
not well.   *Coriolanus*, Act I, sc. 6.

SUICIDE

There is left us ourselves to end ourselves.
Antony and Cleopatra, Act IV, sc. 14.

✦

So every bondman in his own hand bears the power
to cancel his captivity.   *Julius Caesar*, Act I, sc. 3.

✦

Is it sin to rush into the secret house of death, ere
death dare come to us?
Antony and Cleopatra, Act IV, sc. 15.

✦

Against self-slaughter there is a prohibition so divine
that cravens my weak hand.
Cymbeline, Act III, sc. 4.

✦

This mortal house I'll ruin.
Antony and Cleopatra, Act V, sc. 2.

✦

For who would bear the whips and scorns of time,
The oppressor's wrong, the proud man's contumely,
The pangs of despised love, the law's delay,
The insolence of office, and the spurns
That patient merit of the unworthy takes,
When he himself might his quietus make
With a bare bodkin?   *Hamlet*, Act III, sc. 1.

SUSPICION

See what a ready tongue suspicion hath!
Henry IV, Part II, Act I, sc. 1.

Suspicion always haunts the guilty mind; the thief
doth fear each bush an officer.
                    Henry VI, Part III, Act V, sc. 6.

✦

My heart suspects more than mine eye can see.
                    Titus Andronicus, Act II, sc. 3.

✦

Bid Suspicion double-lock the door.
                    Venus and Adonis.

THEATRE

What's Hecuba to him, or he to Hecuba,
That he should weep for her? What would he do,
Had he the motive and the cue for passion
That I have? He would drown the stage with tears.
                    Hamlet, Act II, sc. 2.

✦

Speak the speech, I pray you, as I pronounced it to
you, trippingly on the tongue: but if you mouth it,
as many of your players do, I had as lief the town-
crier spoke my lines.   *Hamlet*, Act III, sc. 2.

✦

Suit the action to the word, the word to the action;
with this special observance, that you o'erstep not
the modesty of nature: for . . . the purpose of play-
ing . . . was and is, to hold, as 'twere, the mirror up
to nature.   *Hamlet*, Act III, sc. 2.

✦

The play's the thing wherein I'll catch the conscience of the king.   *Hamlet*, Act II, sc. 2.

THOUGHT

Make not your thoughts your prisons.
Antony and Cleopatra, Act V, sc. 2.

✦

But thought's the slave of life, and life time's fool.
Henry IV, Part I, Act V, sc. 4.

✦

There is nothing either good or bad, but thinking
makes it so.   *Hamlet*, Act II, sc. 2.

✦

Thoughts are but dreams till their effects be tried.
The Rape of Lucrece.

✦

My thoughts are whirled like a potter's wheel.
Henry VI, Part I, Act 1, sc. 5.

✦

A thought which, quarter'd, hath but one part wisdom and ever three parts coward.
Hamlet, Act IV, sc. 4.

✦

Call home thy ancient thoughts from banishment.
The Taming of the Shrew, Induction, sc. 2.

TIME

Like as the waves make towards the pebbled shore,
So do our minutes hasten to their end.
Sonnet LX.

The whirligig of time brings in his revenges.
Twelfth Night, Act V, sc. 1.

✦

Time is like a fashionable host
That slightly shakes his parting guest by the hand,
And with his arms outstretch'd, as he would fly,
Grasps in the comer.
Troilus and Cressida, Act III, sc. 3.

✦

Time hath, my lord, a wallet at his back
Wherein he puts alms for oblivion,
A great-sized monster of ingratitudes:
Those scraps are good deeds past, which are devour'd
As fast as they are made, forgot as soon as done.
Troilus and Cressida, Act III, sc. 3.

✦

Time's the king of men; he's both their parent, and
he is their grave, and gives them what he will, not
what they crave.
Pericles, Act II, sc. 3.

✦

Time's glory is to calm contending kings,
To unmask falsehood and bring truth to light,
To stamp the seal of time in aged things,
To wake the morn and sentinel the night,
To wrong the wronger till he render right,
To ruinate proud buildings with thy hours
And smear with dust their glittering golden towers.
The Rape of Lucrece.

✦

Nothing 'gainst Time's scythe can make defence.
Sonnet XII.

Ruin has taught me thus to ruminate,
That Time will come and take my love away.
  This thought is as a death, which cannot choose
  But weep to have that which it fears to lose.

Sonnet LXIV.

✦

The extreme parts of time extremely forms all
causes to the purpose of his speed.

Love's Labour's Lost, Act V, sc. 2.

✦

Pleasure and action make the hours seem short.

Othello, Act II, sc. 3.

✦

Short time seems long in sorrow's sharp sustaining.

The Rape of Lucrece.

✦

The time is out of joint: O cursed spite, that ever
I was born to set it right!   *Hamlet*, Act I, sc. 5.

✦

I wasted time, and now doth time waste me.

Richard II, Act V, sc. 5.

TRUTH

Truth is truth to the end of reckoning.

Measure for Measure, Act V, sc. 1.

✦

But wonder on, till truth makes all things plain.

A Midsummer Night's Dream, Act V, sc. 1.

They breathe truth that breathe their words in pain.
Richard II, Act II, sc. 1.

✦

Truth will come to light . . . at the length, the truth
will out.   *The Merchant of Venice*, Act II, sc. 2.

✦

While you live, tell truth, and shame the devil!
Henry IV, Part I, Act III, sc. 1.

✦

But 'tis strange: and oftentimes, to win us to
our harm, the instruments of darkness tell us truths,
win us with honest trifles, to betray's in deepest
consequence.   *Macbeth*, Act I, sc. 3.

✦

Against my soul's pure truth why labour you to
make it wander in an unknown field?
The Comedy of Errors, Act III, sc. 2.

VALOUR

The better part of valour is discretion.
Henry IV, Part I, Act V, sc. 4.

✦

When valour preys on reason, it eats the sword it
fights with.   *Antony and Cleopatra*, Act III, sc. 13.

✦

'Tis much he dares; and, to that dauntless temper of
his mind, he hath a wisdom that doth guide his valour to act in safety.   *Macbeth*, Act III, sc. 1.

He's truly valiant that can wisely suffer
The worst that man can breathe, and make his wrongs
His outsides, to wear them like his raiment, carelessly,
And ne'er prefer his injuries to his heart,
To bring it into danger.
Timon of Athens, Act III, sc. 5.

VARIOUS

An ill-favoured thing, sir, but mine own.
As You Like It, Act V, sc. 4.

✦

Something is rotten in the state of Denmark.
Hamlet, Act I, sc. 4.

✦

Murder most foul, as in the best it is, but this most foul, strange, and unnatural.   *Hamlet*, Act I, sc. 5.

✦

Be thou as chaste as ice, as pure as snow, thou shalt not escape calumny. Get thee to a nunnery, go.
Hamlet, Act III, sc. 1.

✦

The lady doth protest too much, methinks.
Hamlet, Act III, sc. 2.

✦

Never alone did the king sigh, but with a general groan.   *Hamlet*, Act III, sc. 3.

✦

How all occasions do inform against me, and spur my dull revenge!   *Hamlet*, Act IV, sc. 4.

Alas, poor Yorick! I knew him, Horatio: a fellow of infinite jest, of most excellent fancy.
Hamlet, Act V, sc. 1.

◆

Sweets to the sweet: farewell! *Hamlet*, Act V, sc. 1.

◆

A hue and cry hath follow'd certain men unto this house.
Henry IV, Part I, Act II, sc. 4.

◆

We have heard the chimes at midnight.
Henry IV, Part II, Act III, sc. 2.

◆

Once more unto the breach, dear friends, once more, or close the wall up with our English dead!
Henry V, Act III, sc. 1.

◆

Not that I loved Caesar less, but that I loved Rome more.
Julius Caesar, Act III, sc. 2.

◆

This was the most unkindest cut of all.
Julius Caesar, Act III, sc. 2.

◆

This was the noblest Roman of them all.
Julius Caesar, Act V, sc. 5.

◆

Child Rowland to the dark tower came,
His word was still,—Fie, foh, and fum,
I smell the blood of a British man.
King Lear, Act III, sc. 4.

Ripeness is all.   *King Lear*, Act V, sc. 2.

✦

Double, double toil and trouble; fire burn and caul-
dron bubble.   *Macbeth*, Act IV, sc. 1.

✦

Eye of newt and toe of frog, wool of bat and tongue
of dog.   *Macbeth*, Act IV, sc. 1.

✦

By the pricking of my thumbs, something wicked
this way comes.   *Macbeth*, Act IV, sc. 1.

✦

Out, damned spot! out, I say!
         Macbeth, Act V, sc. 1.

✦

All the perfumes of Arabia will not sweeten this little hand.   *Macbeth*, Act V, sc. 1.

✦

I pull in resolution, and begin to doubt the equivocation of the fiend that lies like truth: "Fear not, till
Birnam wood do come to Dunsinane."
         Macbeth, Act V, sc. 5.

✦

What's mine is yours, and what is yours is mine.
         Measure for Measure, Act V, sc. 1.

✦

Are you good men and true?
         Much Ado about Nothing, Act III, sc. 3.

✦

Your daughter and the Moor are now making the
beast with two backs.   *Othello*, Act I, sc. 1.

A horse! a horse! my kingdom for a horse!
Richard III, Act V, sc. 4.

✦

A rose by any other name would smell as sweet.
Romeo and Juliet, Act II, sc. 2.

✦

A plague o' both your houses!
Romeo and Juliet, Act III, sc. 1.

✦

How beauteous mankind is! O brave new world, that has such people in't!
The Tempest, Act V, sc. 1.

WISHES

Thy wish was father . . . to that thought.
Henry IV, Part II, Act IV, sc. 5.

✦

If wishes would prevail with me, my purpose should not fail with me.   *Henry V*, Act III, sc. 2.

✦

Where nothing wants that want itself doth seek.
Love's Labour's Lost, Act IV, sc. 3.

✦

Wishers were ever fools.
Antony and Cleopatra, Act IV, sc. 15.